Library of congress Cataloging-in-Publication Data available

ISBN 978-0-545-82624-2

10 9 8 7 6 5 4 3 2 1   15 16 17 18 19

Printed in the U.S.A. 40
First printing, September 2015
Book design by Kay Petronio

101 ANIMAL SUPER POWERS

BY Melvin + Gilda Berger

Scholastic Inc.

Wild African grey parrots live in flocks and are well known for their natural ability to communicate with one another. Recently, some of these birds have been taught to understand and speak with humans. A parrot named Alex learned to say the names of fifty objects, seven colors, and five shapes! Other parrots were taught to say words and phrases that they heard only a few times. Experts say that someday parrots may learn to count and to read words.

#1 AFRICAN GREY PARROTS TALK

#2 APHIDS MULTIPLY FAST

Aphids are super-powerful producers of offspring. Female aphids are actually born pregnant and every ten days give birth to a new generation of aphids. The newborn females are also pregnant at birth. Generation follows generation, and in just one year, a female—and all her offspring—can create about a *billion* new aphids! These tiny insects need to multiply fast because they have so many enemies, including ladybugs, wasps, spiders, and ants. Predators eat aphids by the hundreds of thousands.

Several species of armadillos have the power to roll themselves into balls. Instead of having fur like other mammals, the armadillos have a body covering of small, hard scales, which protects the animal like a coat of armor. At the first sign of danger, the armadillo dashes into its underground burrow. But if its home is too far away, the armadillo just tucks its legs, tail, and head inside the armor—safe from attack by coyotes and other predators. The armadillo's shell is its best super power.

3 ARMADILLOS ROLL INTO BALLS

4 BALLOONFISH BLOW UP

The bodies of balloonfish are covered with long, sharp, pointed spines. Normally, the spines lie flat on their bodies, offering the fish little protection. But when threatened, balloonfish take in huge gulps of water and, in just a few seconds, become two or three times their usual size! Then, the spines pop up and point straight out from their bodies—like nothing you've ever seen. No predator is tempted to take a bite of a puffed-up, prickly balloonfish.

A barnacle is a shellfish that holds fast to rocks, boats, and solid structures underwater. It begins life as a free-swimming young barnacle, called a larva. After a few months, the larva drops a tiny bit of oil on a rock or other underwater object. The oil clears the water from the surface, and the larva lays down the glue. On this spot, it grows into an adult. The natural superglue holds the barnacle in place for life and even after death—no matter how strong the wind or waves. Now that's some powerful glue!

#5 BARNACLES STICK LIKE SUPERGLUE

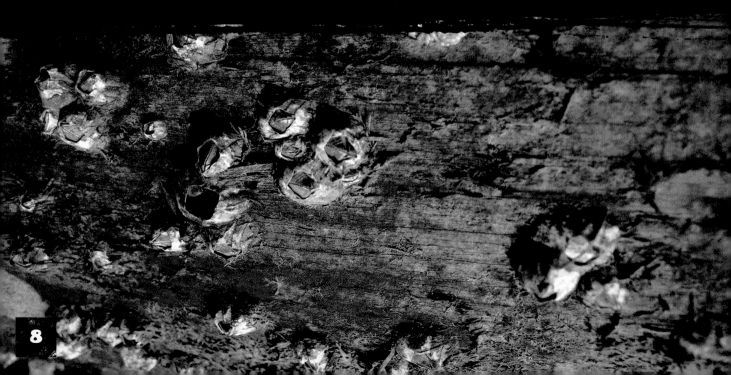

#6 BOA CONSTRICTORS SQUEEZE PREY TO DEATH

Boa constrictors are large snakes and deadly predators. Yet they have no fangs and their bites are not poisonous. Their super power consists of an ability to wrap their long bodies around their victims and squeeze them, harder and harder. As boa contrictors tighten their grip, the prey find it increasingly difficult to breathe. Finally, they choke to death. Deer, wild pigs, monkeys, and lizards all die because of the superior strength of the boa constrictors, which then swallow them whole!

A bombardier beetle is not able to fly away fast enough to escape its enemies. So, to avoid being squashed or eaten, it often attacks at the first sign of danger. The beetle surprises an approaching predator with a blast of boiling-hot, poisonous chemicals from inside its body. The spray explodes out with a loud *POP!* Sometimes, the beetle sprays several times. The noise, the heat, and the pain startle the attacker, while the beetle escapes unharmed.

7 BOMBARDIER BEETLES ATTACK WITH POISON

#8 BOOTLACE WORMS GRAB PREY

A bootlace worm is one of the longest of all animals. At a length of about 100 feet (30 m), it is also a more tangled mess than any worm you may know. But its super power is not its length. It comes from its proboscis, a structure found inside one end of its tube-like body. To capture prey, such as snails, shellfish, or fish, the bootlace worm shoots out its nose-like proboscis. It reaches for its prey with a number of thin, sticky, tiny "fingers" at the end of its "nose." In seconds, the prey becomes the worm's next meal!

Burrowing owls make their nests in burrows, or tunnels, that they find or dig in the ground. They then collect dung, the poop from cattle or horses, and spread it around the entrance to the burrow. This bait attracts insects, especially dung beetles, the burrowing owl's favorite food. The beetles collect the dung, which they roll into big balls to eat later. But once they are at the owls' burrow, the tricky birds snatch up the beetles—just like food delivered to their door!

9 BURROWING OWLS PLAY TRICKS

#10 BUTTERFLIES TASTE WITH THEIR FEET

A butterfly flies from flower to flower to drink nectar, a liquid found inside most flowers. The butterfly places its feet on the flower. Taste buds, called chemoreceptors, on the bottom of its feet pick up information about the food. They flash back a message to the brain that the nectar is either good or not good to eat. If it is fit for eating, the butterfly unrolls its long tongue and sucks it up. A female butterfly also uses her super-power feet when seeking the best place to lay her eggs.

Some catfish live deep under the sea, where there is no light and very little food. This makes it hard for catfish to find bristle worms, their favorite prey, which are hidden in the ocean bottom. As the worms breathe underwater, however, they give out tiny amounts of carbon dioxide, which slightly changes the water's acidity. Using its whiskers, a catfish picks up the slightest difference in the chemistry of the water. And the catfish finds the worm—even in the dark!

11 CATFISH WHISKERS SPOT PREY

#12 CHAMELEONS MOVE ONE EYE AT A TIME

Chameleons are best known for being able to change skin color. But even more astounding is their super eyesight. Each of their two eyes sticks out from the head and is covered by a rounded eyelid with a small opening. And each eye can turn or rotate on its own! With this power, a chameleon can look forward and backward at the same time. It can hunt for insects to eat while looking out for danger. Once it has found prey or predator, it can focus both eyes to see it more clearly.

Chipmunks are super-powerful diggers! They dig tunnels, or burrows, in which they live. They are well equipped with extra-strong bones in all four legs, super-sharp front claws, and very hard nose pads. A chipmunk first makes a burrow opening with its head and nose. Then, with a swimming motion, it uses the claws on its front and rear feet to fling the dirt behind its body. Finally, it turns around and, like a bulldozer, pushes the dirt out of the burrow. Now it has a safe place to live and store its food!

#13 CHIPMUNKS DIG TUNNELS

#14 CLAMS DIG WITH A FOOT

Clams live on ocean bottoms and along the shores of oceans, lakes, and streams. The clam's body is completely covered by a shell made up of two parts, with a small muscle that opens and closes the shell. Inside the clam's body is a large, muscular organ, called a foot. The clam reaches out with the foot to burrow, or dig, in the mud or sand. Sometimes, a clam is thrown out of the water by a wave or tide. Then, it uses its powerful foot to help it get back into the water. Water flows in and out two other openings to bring the clam its food.

Some cockroaches can fly—but ALL can run fast. In fact, cockroaches hold the title as one of the world's fastest-running insects! They mostly stay out of sight during the day and only come out of their hiding places after dark. Flip on a light—and they dart away. Their super-speedy nervous system carries warning signals around their body ten times faster than your nerves do. When a cockroach senses danger, a message travels from brain to legs quicker than the blink of an eye!

15 COCKROACHES RACE FROM DANGER

#16 CROCODILES LOCK THEIR JAWS

Crocodiles bite with the most powerful force of any living animal! A hunting crocodile hides and waits out of sight, ready to lunge at its prey. When the crocodile attacks, its jaws fly open and quickly slam shut on the victim. The two parts of the jaw lock so that the fish, bird, turtle, or other prey is firmly trapped between them. The crocodile then drags and rolls the prey under the water until it drowns. Few animals can escape an attack by one of these mighty predators.

Male deer, called bucks, grow big, hard, bony antlers on their skulls. All antlers have branches that end in points and give bucks incredible power. Antlers are a male deer's weapon in case of attack. But mostly, bucks use them to fight other males in the group. The strongest buck, rather than the one with the biggest antlers, is recognized as most important and becomes leader of the herd. Sometimes, just pretending and threatening to use his antlers is enough to avoid a fight and win the battle with another buck.

#17 DEER BATTLE WITH THEIR ANTLERS

#18 DOGS FOLLOW SCENT TRAILS

A dog's super-keen sense of smell is about tens of thousands of times sharper than that of a human! It can recognize as many as 100,000 different kinds of odors! Some dogs are able to follow scent trails that are more than four days old and many miles long. Such dogs have been known to trace a trail, even under snow, through cities and over mountains. All in all, a dog has about forty times more brainpower devoted to smell than you do—even though its brain is much smaller than yours.

Draco lizards are often called flying dragons, even though they don't actually fly. They glide from tree to tree. Large flaps of skin are folded on the sides of the lizard's body. To get from one tree to another, the lizard opens the flaps to form "wings." When it jumps, the wings catch the wind and carry the lizard as far as 30 feet (9 m). That's about the distance from one side of a tennis court to the other. After all, gliding through air is far safer than scampering across a forest floor!

19 DRACO LIZARDS GLIDE

#20 DRAGONFLY EYES SEE ALL AROUND

A dragonfly has among the biggest eyes of all insects. Its two huge eyes, which look like round beads, completely cover its head. Each eye, called a compound eye, is made up of about 30,000 separate lenses. Compare that with humans, who have only one lens in each eye. With thousands of lenses, the insect can see super well, near and far, and in all directions—up and down, from side to side, and forward and backward! Compound eyes are super useful for catching prey AND escaping danger.

Dung beetles take their name from their very unusual habit of eating dung, the poop of large animals. And of all the different kinds of dung that they eat, lab tests show, this beetle's favorite comes from chimpanzees. To get their food, the beetles collect bits of dung and roll them into enormous balls with their feet. The balls, sometimes 1,000 times their weight, often tower over the small bugs. Then the beetles push and pull the giant balls back to their burrows—to be enjoyed later. Female beetles also lay their eggs in balls of dung.

#21 DUNG BEETLES PULL 1,000 TIMES THEIR WEIGHT

#22 EAGLES SPOT PREY FAR AWAY

Eagles are birds of prey that can see four to five times better than humans—and usually more clearly. If you had eagle eyes, you could see an ant crawling on the ground from the roof of a ten-story building! Even though an eagle's eyes are on the sides of its head, it can see forward as well as all around. While soaring high in the sky or from a perch closer to the ground, an eagle can spot a rabbit in a field or a fish in water.

Being able to breathe under the ground is an earthworm's super power. An earthworm does not have a nose or lungs. Instead, it takes in air through its thin skin. Its body picks up tiny bubbles of air that are trapped in the soil. Since air will only pass through skin that is moist, an earthworm avoids sunlight and other drying effects. When it rains, though, the ground above gets moist. Then earthworms come up out of their tunnels because they can crawl along wet surfaces more easily than through soil.

23 EARTHWORMS BREATHE THROUGH THEIR SKIN

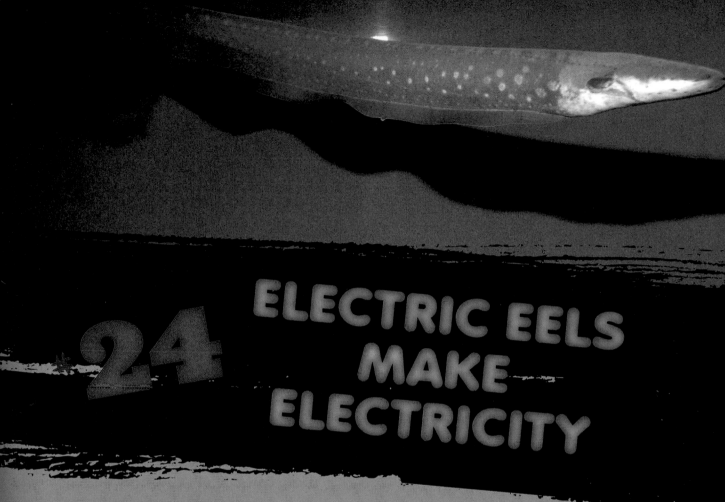

ELECTRIC EELS MAKE ELECTRICITY

24

Electric eels can produce electric currents as high as 600 volts underwater! That's five times as strong as the voltage from a North American electric outlet. Most of their bodies are lined with cells, called electrocytes. Each one is like a tiny battery. As the electric eel swims, it emits pulses of weak electrical current that scans its surroundings, like radar. When the eel detects a fish, it sends out a burst of high-voltage power, stunning the prey and making it easy to snatch.

An elephant's trunk is super-powered. It's a nose for breathing and smelling, but it is also vitally important in other ways. About 5 feet (1.5 m) long and 300 pounds (136 kg) in weight, the trunk makes the elephant one of the strongest of all animals. Using its trunk, the elephant can carry a log that weighs as much as 600 pounds (272 kg). The elephant can wrap its trunk around a big tree and pull it out of the ground. With one swat of its trunk, it can break an enemy's bones.

25 ELEPHANT TRUNKS LIFT AND CARRY

#26 EUROPEAN ROBINS MIGRATE WITH A BUILT-IN COMPASS

A European robin has a compass in its head that senses the earth's magnetism. It is a fact not discovered until 1968. The robin is among the last birds to fly south in the autumn and the first to return north in the spring. Often, it returns to the same place every year. Why doesn't it get lost? Its built-in compass guides it along the way! The robin actually sees the earth's magnetism as a map of light and dark patches. As it flies, the "map" is always changing, keeping the robin, and other birds with compasses, on course!

29

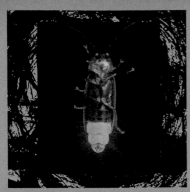

Fireflies, also called lightning bugs, produce short bursts of light, called bioluminescence. They do this by bringing together two chemicals in their bodies. Other insects and some fish also have the power to produce light. But fireflies are among the few animals that can flash the light on and off in distinct signals. Males send out their patterns of light bursts. Females answer with their patterns. Back and forth the fireflies signal, until the insects come together to mate.

27 FIREFLIES SIGNAL WITH LIGHT

28 FLIES SENSE DANGER

A fly has two antennae and many short hairs on its body that sense the slightest movement of the air around it. That's why when someone starts to swat a fly, the insect immediately feels the air moving. It can even tell the direction the danger is coming from. In a fraction of a second, the fly takes off—in the opposite direction—flapping its wings at an amazing 200 times a second. It makes its high-speed escape, twisting and turning in the air to elude the attacker.

Flying gurnards are fish that live in shallow ocean waters. Although they can swim, they usually walk along the sandy bottoms, looking for food. But a flying gurnard quickly changes appearance when alarmed or threatened by a predator. The fish spreads its two large pectoral fins and shoots forward at high speed, taking quick, short flights through the water. With pectoral fins extended, the flying gurnard looks much larger than usual—and far scarier.

29 FLYING GURNARDS CHANGE SHAPE

#30 FLYING SQUIRRELS SOAR LIKE KITES

A flying squirrel actually moves through the air like a glider or a kite. Folds of skin that grow between its front and back legs can form wings. As the squirrel takes off, it stretches out its four legs and opens the folds. With wings spread out, the squirrel soars forward, held up by the air. It moves its tail to steer and to avoid crashing into tree trunks or hanging branches. One glide can carry a flying squirrel farther than half the length of a football field!

A frogfish has a bone that looks like a fishing line sticking out from its head. At the end of the line, a worm-like lure dangles in front of the frogfish's mouth. When hunting, the frogfish usually stays still in one place and waits for prey to swim by. Sometimes, it wiggles the lure to attract fish, crabs, or shrimp. Seeing the "worm," the prey comes closer. In a flash, the frogfish flings open its huge mouth and sucks in the prey. Frogfish are thought to gulp down food faster than any other animal.

#31 FROGFISH GO FISHING

32 FROGS SEE THROUGH A THIRD EYELID

Frogs have two eyelids, just as you do, plus a very important third eyelid on each eye. The third eyelids are transparent, or see-through, and, like goggles, protect the frog's eyes in many ways. While swimming underwater, a frog sees more clearly when looking for food or avoiding danger. Out of water, a frog's eyes stay moist longer and free of dirt or blowing sand. And when moving between land and water, the frog's third eyelids prevent any blurring of vision, so they can steer clear of predators.

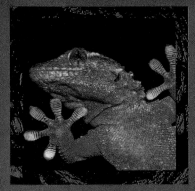

Geckos can walk upside down on smooth surfaces because of their amazing feet. Each toe is covered by a pad with many ridges topped with thousands of teeny, tiny hairs. There is only a small attraction between the molecules of the hairs and the molecules of the smooth surface. But the great number of hairs creates a pull that is powerful enough to hold the gecko onto almost anything—even after it dies. To unstick the hairs quickly, the gecko just changes the angle of its foot. Presto! It's done!

#33 GECKOS WALK ACROSS CEILINGS

#34 GORILLAS "SPEAK" WITHOUT WORDS

Gorillas are masters of communication. They grunt and bark to keep the group, or band, together. They scream or roar to alert others to danger. They burp when they're relaxed while eating or resting. And the young cry like human babies when troubled and chuckle at play. Gestures also carry information. Beating the chest warns others away. Staring means they're ready to fight. And an open mouth with bared teeth shows fear. For gorillas, sounds and actions surely speak louder than words!

Grasshoppers have very long, strong back legs that make them incredible jumpers. If a grown man had that much power for his size, he could leap as high as a five-story building! The grasshopper's great jumping ability comes from its two back legs. When ready to leap, the grasshopper tightens the back-leg muscles—and then relaxes them. Just like a giant spring, the action provides a huge release of energy. The grasshopper shoots up and away!

35 GRASSHOPPERS JUMP TWENTY TIMES THEIR BODY LENGTH

36 GRAY WHALES SWIM GREAT DISTANCES

Gray whales swim many thousands of miles every year—probably more than any other mammal. In fall, their travels take them from the cold northern waters of Alaska to the warmer waters of Mexico in the south. In summer, they go back again. Round-trip, the whales log about 12,430 miles (20,000 km)! They stay under the water for up to fifteen minutes at a time and travel at an average speed of about 4 miles per hour (6.4 kph), which is about as fast as you walk. The gray whales take about two to three months to swim each way.

Green anoles are small lizards with one amazing super power: when a predator bites off the end of its tail, a green anole can grow a new piece! The tail section that is chopped off falls to the ground and thrashes about for several minutes. The movement confuses and distracts the attacker. This gives the green anole a chance to escape. Slowly, a new length of tail starts to grow and take the place of the old one. In about two months, the tail is complete again—but usually smaller than the original.

#37 GREEN ANOLES GROW NEW TAILS

#38 GREEN HERONS CATCH FISH WITH BAIT

The green heron is one of the few birds with the power and intelligence to use tools. When hunting for prey, it drops bits of food from its mouth onto the water. They may be breadcrumbs, insects, berries, worms, or even twigs or feathers. Then, the green heron waits at the water's edge, where it hides amid the leafy shrubbery. Sooner or later, a fish comes along, attracted by the bait in the water. As soon as it gets near, the heron lunges forward and surprises the prey with a quick grab of its knife-like bill!

A guinea pig has the amazing ability to keep its four long front teeth as sharp as carving knives! The teeth grow continuously throughout the guinea pig's life at a rate of 3–7 inches (7.6–17.8 cm) a year. As it feeds on hay, grass, fresh fruits, vegetables, and other foods that need lots of chewing, the tops of its teeth grind together, leaving the edges very sharp. Owners often give pet guinea pigs wooden chews or toys to gnaw on, which also help to trim the teeth. Caged guinea pigs have been known to use their sharp teeth for fighting.

39 GUINEA PIG TEETH CUT LIKE KNIVES

#40 HAIRY FROGS BREAK THEIR TOES

When in danger, hairy frogs have the startling power to break their own toes! Sharp pieces of bone push out through the skin on their feet to form cat-like claws. Armed with these pointed claws, the hairy frogs are able to fight off their enemies or get a better grip on rocks as they flee. In time, the frogs' skin grows back and covers the bones. Or sometimes, the bones draw back into the body. Small wonder hairy frogs are also called horror frogs!

Hammerhead sharks, like all other sharks, find prey by sensing the tiny bits of electricity given off by living creatures. But while other sharks hunt with sight, sound, or smell, the hammerhead mainly swings its very wide head back and forth to pick up electrical signals in the water. The many, nearly invisible, black holes that cover its snout and the underside of its head contain nerve endings. They detect even the slightest electrical currents from a prey—which soon becomes the hammerhead's dinner.

#41 HAMMERHEAD SHARKS SENSE ELECTRICAL SIGNALS

#42 HAWK MOTH CATERPILLARS MIMIC SNAKES

Hawk moth caterpillars have a super power known as mimicry. Even though they are very small, these caterpillars imitate larger, fiercer-looking animals to escape danger. When threatened by a bird or other predator, this caterpillar puffs up its body, making its head much bigger and more frightening than normal. At the same time, it hides its legs and reveals two dark spots that look like snake eyes. Such mimicry is often good enough to send the enemy flying!

Hoatzin young, called chicks, have wings but cannot yet fly. This makes it difficult for these tropical birds to escape danger. But they have a secret weapon that helps the chicks survive until their wings grow feathers. It is a claw at the end of each wing! The chicks live in trees overhanging swamps or other water. When a predator attacks, the chick grabs onto tree branches with its claws and clambers away. If the attack continues, the young bird simply dives into the water from the overhanging branches. When safe, it climbs back up the tree with the help of its claws.

43 HOATZIN YOUNG ESCAPE WITH WING CLAWS

HOGNOSE SNAKES PLAY DEAD

44

Hognose snakes are like actors that perform different roles. When attacked by a predator, the snake puts on a show that makes it seem much more dangerous than it really is. The hognose hisses, lunges forward, and spreads open its hood. But if this does not deter the enemy, the snake acts out its most famous role. It plays dead! The snake rolls onto its back, drops open its mouth, and gives off a disgusting smell. Few predators eat dead prey. So they leave the snake alone.

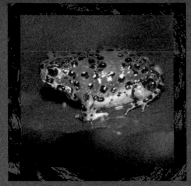

The holy cross toad, also called the crucifix frog, has special glands in its skin. If frightened, its glands leak a sticky fluid that hardens into very strong glue. In seconds, anything or anyone that touches the toad's skin gets stuck fast. This discourages the toad's main predators, snakes and birds, from attacking. But the glue also serves another purpose. It traps in place ants or other insects that crawl onto the toad's body. Later, the toad sheds its skin—and dines on the insects that are stuck there.

#45 HOLY CROSS TOADS OOZE SUPERGLUE

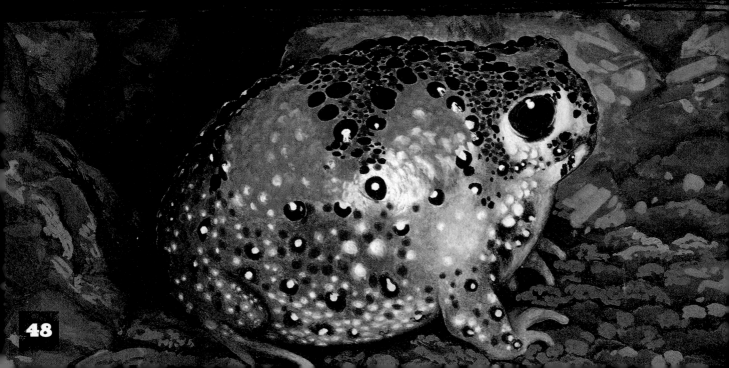

#46 HONEY BADGERS FIGHT WITHOUT FEAR

A honey badger is no bigger than an average dog, yet it will fight animals as large as a lion, leopard, or rhino. Honey badgers have been seen driving a whole pride of lions away from a kill—and then eating it themselves! Armed with strong, sharp teeth and powerful jaws, a single honey badger gives off an awful smell that chokes both predators and prey. When grabbed by its thick, loose, baggy skin, a honey badger twists around and bites. Attackers, beware!

A horned lizard, also known as a horned toad, has a coat of spiny armor to protect it from attacking animals. But when needed, it has an even more powerful defense: it builds up the blood pressure in its head. This causes a stream of blood to shoot out from the side of its eye! It aims the blood, which can travel the length of a car, straight at the wolf, coyote, or other predator. When struck by the blood, the startled and confused enemy usually gives up the attack.

#47 HORNED LIZARDS SQUIRT BLOOD

48 HOWLER MONKEYS GRASP WITH THEIR TAILS

The howler monkey gets its super power from its tail. For this animal, which spends most of its life in the trees, the tail is like an extra arm. It grasps the branches as the monkey clambers through the trees. A patch of bare skin on the bottom side of the tail helps the monkey get a good grip on tree limbs or hang from the branches. The howler rarely leaps or jumps through the trees. Instead, it uses its strong tail to hold on as it collects leaves—its main food.

A hummingbird is a tiny creature—a little longer than a credit card—from tip of bill to tip of tail. Yet it can perform the most difficult gymnastic feats in the air. Using acrobatics, speed, and hovering in space, hummingbirds find food and outwit predators. Twisting and turning, the birds can fly forward, backward, or even upside down. They can also dive at speeds as high as 60 miles per hour (96 kph) and catch insects in mid-flight! Equally amazing is their ability to hover like tiny helicopters as they suck the sugary nectar from flowers.

#49 HUMMINGBIRDS DO ACROBATICS

#50 HUMPBACK WHALES SING LOVE SONGS

A humpback whale sings long "songs" made up of grunts, moans, squeals, clicks, and cries. These songs repeat the same theme or pattern over and over again, for hours or days. The songs themselves change from year to year. Some of them are love songs, which are sung by male humpbacks to attract mates. Other songs are feeding calls that communicate with different whales while they are hunting for fish. All love and feeding songs can be heard up to 10,000 miles (16,093 km) away!

Ibex have the unique ability to climb over steep, rocky cliffs and go where few other animals dare to go. Found in the highest mountain ranges of Europe and Asia, ibex avoid predators by gracefully leaping over treacherous terrain to escape. Often, this puts them outside the range of such enemies as bears, leopards, foxes, and wolves. Soft elastic pads on their hooves help ibex climb into places where there is no solid footing. The pads give ibex a better grip on the ground and rocks and allow them to escape quickly when necessary.

51 IBEX DEFY DANGER

#52 JEWEL BEETLES FLY INTO FIRE

Jewel beetles do not avoid fire like most other animals. Instead, they spread their wings and fly straight toward the blaze! Tiny pits on their bodies can "smell" a fire from as far away as 50 miles (80 km) and guide them in that direction. After the fire scorches the trees, the fire beetles breed and lay their eggs in the burned wood. Because predators run away from fire, no other animals or insects are around to harm the eggs. Also, the newborn beetles can safely feed on a great supply of charred trees.

A jumping spider has eight super-powerful eyes. Four of them face forward. Two enormous eyes give the spider clear, sharp vision, and six smaller eyes spot the slightest movement. All the eyes move in and out to improve focus and turn in any direction—up and down, right and left. With so many amazing eyes, jumping spiders stalk their prey and pounce— and almost always nab their insect victims! According to experts, these animals are among the smartest spiders. Camera companies are now trying to make lenses that "see" as well as jumping spiders do!

#53 JUMPING SPIDERS SEE ALL

#54 KANGAROO TAILS WORK LIKE LEGS

A kangaroo has two long hind legs and two short front legs. But for hopping, it just uses its hind legs, plus its long, muscular tail. The tail is a kind of third leg that adds energy to the hop and also helps with balance; the kangaroo is the only animal with this super power. Extra-strong muscles in the hind legs and tail shoot the kangaroo forward and up, like a spring that gets pressed down and then released. As the kangaroo lands, its hind legs and tail press down again and release. This powers the next jump—and so on.

Komodo dragons are giant lizards with a powerful way of bringing down their prey. The lizard stands still and waits for its meal, such as a monkey, to come along. When the monkey is within reach, the lizard rears up, grabs it, and bites. This delivers a powerful dose of deadly venom, or poison, into the wound. Then, the lizard lets go. It follows its prey as the venom takes effect. Blood streams out of its victim's large, painful wound, and in a little while, the victim stops moving and dies. The Komodo dragon moves in for its dinner—risk-free!

#55 KOMODO DRAGONS HAVE DEADLY BITES

#56 LYREBIRDS ARE COPYCATS

Lyrebirds are super mimics—and have the best vocal cords of any bird. They can repeat almost any sound they hear, from bird songs to car horns! The male lyrebird sings beautiful songs to woo its mate. But mixed in with the songs are sounds that it picks up from its surroundings. They range from fire alarms to chain saws, from radio music to barking dogs, and even human speech! The female lyrebird also sings and copies sounds but is not heard nearly as often as the males.

The mantis shrimp has two super-powerful, club-like claws on the front of its body. These shoot out from the shrimp like bullets from a rifle—and can kill prey. If you could move your arm that fast, you could throw a baseball into outer space! These claws smash the shells and rip the flesh of crab, oyster, and octopus prey with deadly force. Coupled with its killing ability, the mantis shrimp has the most complex eyes of any animal.

#57 MANTIS SHRIMP PACK POWERFUL PUNCHES

#58 MARINE TOADS DRIP POISON

The marine toad, despite its name, spends its entire life on land, not in the water. When confronted by a predator, the animal oozes a thick, milky venom, or poison, onto its skin. The venom comes from two large glands on the giant toad's shoulders. A dose of the venom kills or sickens any animal that tries to eat the toad. It irritates the skin of any human that touches it. Tribal hunters in South America dip their arrows in the venom to make them more deadly.

The word *millipede* means thousand-legged, but that is an exaggeration. Millipedes are small, worm-like animals, with only hundreds, not thousands, of legs. Most millipedes are no bigger than your thumb, yet are powerful enough to discourage predators far larger than themselves. When in danger, some millipedes curl up to protect their legs. At the same time, a bad-smelling poisonous liquid seeps out onto their skin. The chemical tastes bad and is strong enough to sometimes kill, or at least to drive an enemy away.

59 MILLIPEDES OOZE POISON

60 MIMIC OCTOPUSES CHANGE THEIR LOOKS

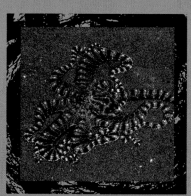

The mimic octopus has one super-powerful way to defend itself. It mimics, or imitates, the look of another animal that its predators find far more dangerous. In one well-known disguise, the mimic octopus changes its appearance to look like a poisonous sea snake, which most of its enemies fear. The octopus hides six of its arms and leaves its other two arms outstretched to mimic the snake. One glance at the sea snake look-alike—and the predator leaves the octopus alone.

Net-casting spiders make webs of silk to trap prey, just like other spiders. But their super power is the way they use the webs to capture prey. The spider hangs head down over a spot where prey often pass. It grasps the four corners of the web with its long legs—and waits. When an insect approaches, the spider drops the clingy web. This entangles the unlucky bug in the silk threads. Quickly, then, the spider lowers itself to grab and devour its catch.

#61 NET-CASTING SPIDERS DROP WEBS

#62 OARFISH SWIM VERTICALLY

Oarfish are special in a few ways: they are among the longest of all fish; they have no scales; and they have no teeth. But their most amazing power is the ability to swim straight up or straight down, instead of horizontally, like most fish! Oarfish live in deep water at the bottom of the world's oceans. By swimming head up and face down at great speeds, the oarfish finds the small fish and shrimp it feeds on. Also, it can escape sharks and other enemies that swim the usual way.

Octopuses escape their enemies by spraying thick clouds of dark ink into the water as they flee. Each kind of octopus has a different color ink. The ink makes the water so murky that predators, such as seals, whales, and sharks, cannot see the octopus. The ink also contains a toxic compound that irritates a predator's eyes. Sometimes, the cloud looks like the octopus itself. The predator attacks it, while the real octopus makes its getaway. The ink may also hide the smell of the octopus, making it harder for a predator to track.

#63 OCTOPUSES SQUIRT INK

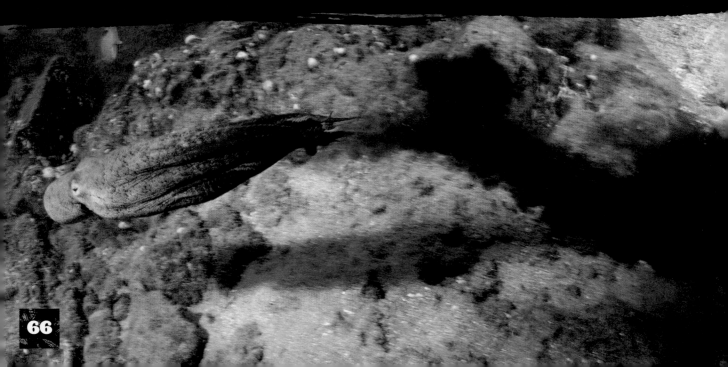

#64 PARROTFISH WEAR "PAJAMAS"

Parrotfish are active during the day and rest at night. During their resting time, some parrotfish wrap themselves in a kind of see-through envelope, open at both ends. People often call the nighttime covering "pajamas." It smells and tastes bad, which may keep away predators that hunt by scent. The pajamas may also hide the smell of the parrotfish, making it harder for nighttime hunters, like moray eels and sharks, to find them. No one knows for sure.

Peregrine falcons hunt for prey from extremely high cliffs, mountains, or skyscrapers. When diving down to catch a bird in midair, the falcon can reach a record-breaking speed of about 200 miles per hour (322 kph)! At that speed, it is probably the fastest of all animals. While taking the deep plunge, called a stoop, the peregrine falcon holds its head straight up to keep its prey in view. After stunning the victim with a blow of its feet, the falcon swings around and grabs the bird. Sometimes, it even starts to eat it—while still in flight!

#65 PEREGRINE FALCONS POWER-DIVE

#66 PIPEFISH HIDE

The pipefish is mainly protected from larger fish enemies by its shape and color. Its long, slim body blends in easily with weeds and grass growing in the water. Since its body matches the green sea plants, is vertical, and sways gently, the pipefish is hard to see. Actually, this fish has few other ways to defend itself. It swims slowly because of its small fins and stiff body, gets very little protection from its scales, and is unable to open its mouth to fight back. Camouflage is its greatest power!

Pistol shrimp are tiny, finger-sized creatures that hold open their claws while hunting. One of the pistol shrimp's claws is much larger than the other, with a trigger like a pistol. When a pistol shrimp spots its prey, it cocks the trigger. Then, it quickly slams shut its claw—NOT to grab its prey but to create a bubble of boiling-hot water almost as hot as the surface of the sun! When the bubble pops, it makes a bang louder than the sound of a gun being fired—which gives the shrimp its name. The incredibly loud noise stuns any nearby prey—and the pistol shrimp moves in for the kill.

67 PISTOL SHRIMP HUNT WITH SOUND

#68 PIT VIPERS SENSE BODY HEAT

The pit viper has many extremely sensitive sensors that detect heat. The sensors are located in openings, or pit holes, found in front of each eye. They can pick up body heat given off by other animals as far as 3 feet (.9 m) away. The heat forms a 3-D picture in the snake's brain, much as light from an object forms an image in your brain. This "heat vision" lets the pit viper see the animal in the dark, when it is active. Then, the snake either attacks the prey or quickly escapes.

The platypus bill contains nearly 40,000 cells that detect electricity. The electrical signals come from the activity of the nerves and muscles present in all living beings. As a platypus hunts, with its eyes, ears, and nostrils closed, the skin on its bill senses the electrical signals from any nearby animals. With this sixth sense, the platypus finds its food—fish, shrimp, and other creatures that live in the water. Once it detects the electricity, it uses its sense of touch to zero in on the prey and enjoy its next meal—without ever having seen, heard, or smelled it!

#69 PLATYPUS BILLS PICK UP ELECTRICAL SIGNALS

#70 POLAR BEARS SMELL FOOD MILES AWAY

Polar bears are able to sniff out seals and other prey that are up to 20 miles (32 km) away, or hidden under 3 feet (.9 m) of ice! They also find seals at holes in the ice, when the seals come up for air. In places where the ice has broken up, polar bears seek out seals as they rest on floating sheets of ice. In the spring, they detect seals in their dens, which are often buried under layers of snow. Polar bears also use their most powerful sense of smell to find dead whales, another favorite food.

A porcupine is protected by long, strong bristles of hair, called quills, which are loosely attached to its body and tail. Altogether, a porcupine may have tens of thousands of quills. The needle-like hairs, with barbs at the end, lie flat until a porcupine is under attack. Then, the animal raises them. When predators brush up against the porcupine, the quills come out easily. Often, they get stuck in the attacker's skin. Sometimes, the porcupine smacks a bobcat or other enemy with its quill-covered tail. Ouch! But don't worry—the quills will grow back again.

71 PORCUPINES RAISE THEIR QUILLS

#72 PRONGHORNS RUN MARATHONS

Pronghorns are the fastest land mammals in North America—even faster than African cheetahs over long distances. The pronghorns can run about 30 miles per hour (48 kph) for over 20 miles (32 km)—and have been known to go twice that fast on short runs. No other animal has the endurance of the pronghorn. Its speed and stamina allow it to escape coyotes, wolves, and other predators. On the open prairies, where they live, running is a pronghorn's most outstanding power.

A rabbit mother, called a doe, takes exceptional care of her young. The doe makes a nest for them in a shallow hole, or burrow, that she digs in the ground. The babies, called kits, cannot see or hear and have no fur. She lines the nest and covers the helpless kits with clumps of fur that she rips from her chest. To the fur, she adds blades of grass to keep the kits warm and to hide them from predators. She nurses and guards them until they are able to live on their own and leave the nest.

#73 RABBIT MOTHERS RIP THEIR FUR FOR NESTS

#74 RATS SMELL IN "STEREO"

A rat is said to smell in stereo because its two nostrils pick up separate sources of odors. The brain can then locate the direction and distance to the smell. A rat's ability to smell is similar to the way your two ears hear sounds independently and give you the direction and distance of a sound. A strong smell in the right nostril, for example, tells the rat the smell came from that direction and is close. Stereo smell lets a rat sniff out danger—and find the cheese!

Ounce for ounce, the rhinoceros beetle is the world's strongest creature—far stronger than a full-grown elephant! As a measure of its power, lab tests show that a rhinoceros beetle can carry 850 times its weight on its back! This beetle, one of the largest in the world, may grow up to 7 inches (18 cm) long. The beetle uses its incredible might to battle other males for mates. It also puts its great force to work, digging in the jungle floor to escape predators. For good reason, the lowly rhinoceros beetle is named after the colossal rhinoceros.

#75 RHINOCEROS BEETLES BATTLE RIVALS

76 RUPPELL'S GRIFFONS BREATHE THIN AIR

Ruppell's griffons are the highest-flying birds in the world. They fly a spectacular 7 miles (11 km) above the earth to spot—and eat—dead animals on the ground. At this height, the air is said to be thin because it contains very little oxygen. Passenger planes flying at that altitude provide more oxygen by raising the air pressure in the cabin. Yet, the Ruppell's griffons breathe without difficulty. Thanks to a special protein in their blood, they make the best use of the little oxygen available at great heights.

The sawfish has a "saw," from which it takes its name. The saw is a long, flat snout lined with lots of small teeth, called denticles. When the sawfish finds a school of fish, it swings the saw from side to side, much like a sword in the hands of a fighter. This back-and-forth slashing leaves many herring or other fish dead, injured, or stunned and ready to be seized and eaten. When not slashing, the sawfish uses its saw to rake the ocean bottom for shellfish and other prey.

#77 SAWFISH SLASH PREY

#78 SCALLOPS SEE IN DARK WATER

Few people know that scallops have many tiny, bright blue eyes along the inside edge of their shells. Each eye has many little mirrors on the back of the retina, called tapeta. The tapeta bounce light back onto the retina—much as they do in the eyes of cats, raccoons, and other animals. This makes dim light appear brighter. They let scallops tell light from dark and detect any movement in the water. Best of all, they warn of danger—in time for scallops to shut their shells.

Seals are able to track prey fish by pursuing the invisible trails they leave in the water. The seals use their highly sensitive whiskers to follow the underwater disturbances left by the fish, much as bloodhounds sniff people's scents on land. And seals can detect the trails up to half a minute after the fish have passed! Scientists tell us that seals use this super power to track down prey in dark or dirty water. The water trails can even tell seals the size and speed of the fish they are tracking.

#79 SEALS FOLLOW WATER TRAILS

80 SNAKES SMELL WITH THEIR TONGUES

A snake flicks its forked tongue in and out to pick up smells in the air—even without opening its mouth. Its tongue, which passes through a notch in the upper lip, also tastes objects it can touch. When the snake pulls its tongue back into the mouth, a message travels from a sense organ, known as Jacobson's organ, to the brain. This tells the snake if a dangerous predator is approaching.

Sperm whales dive several thousand feet under the water in search of food, mainly squid. They can stay underwater for an hour and a half—or longer—without taking a breath! Compare that with most humans, who can't hold their breath for more than a minute or two. The whales' ability to hold their breath for such a long time comes from a special substance in their blood. The substance stores extra oxygen and makes a single breath of air go a long, long way!

#81 SPERM WHALES DIVE DEEP

#82 SPIDERS PLUCK THEIR WEBS

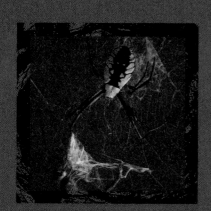

Most everyone knows that spiders build webs to trap bugs for food. But new studies show that spiders gather information about the bug once it's in the web. The spider plucks the web's silk threads—similar to the way a person strums a guitar. The spider's legs pick up the web's vibrations and send messages to its brain on the exact location, size, and weight of the entangled animal. Now the spider can decide whether the animal is prey, predator, or, perhaps, a mate.

Spitting spiders are small and have the spiders' usual eight legs. Despite being nearly blind, they are very clever hunters. They can catch and kill insects with a stream of sticky spit! A spitting spider looks for prey at night. Once it spots a victim, the spider sneaks up and spits a sticky silky substance over it. Larger prey may require the spider to spit several times. The spit pins down the prey so that it cannot move. But before eating it, the spider scurries over, bites the insect, and injects even more poison.

83 SPITTING SPIDERS KILL

84 SPITTLEBUG YOUNG PROTECT THEMSELVES

Female spittlebugs lay eggs on the stems of grasses and other plants. The eggs hatch into tiny young, called nymphs. It is the stage just before becoming an adult. A nymph spits out enough white, frothy, bubbly liquid, called spittle, to cover and surround its entire body. Often, more than one nymph hides inside the mass of spittle. The spittle prevents the nymphs from drying out in hot weather and shelters the young from attacks by insects and birds.

A squid swims by a kind of jet action. The animal fills its body with water, which it then shoots out through a thin tube, or funnel, that lies beneath its head. The fast-moving water rushing out the back end of the funnel sends the squid forward. It is the same as gas shooting out the back of a plane's jet engine to push the plane forward. The squid steers by changing the direction of the funnel. Jet action lets squids reach up to 25 miles an hour (40 kph)!

#85 SQUID JET THROUGH WATER

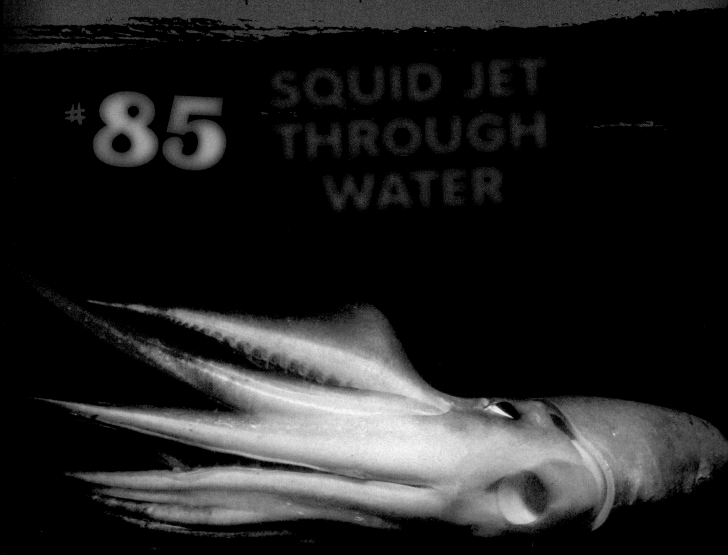

#86 STARFISH PRY OPEN CLAMSHELLS

A starfish, or sea star (since it is not a fish), usually has five arms. The underside has its mouth and many small tubes, called tube feet, for walking and finding food. The feet have suction disks at the ends. When the starfish finds a clam, its tube feet attach to the shell and slowly pry it open. Then, the starfish pushes its stomach out through its mouth and into the clamshell! Here it slowly digests the clam's body. Finally, the starfish pulls back its stomach—and the empty clamshell drops away.

Star-nosed moles, with their bizarre star-shaped nose, live near wetlands, marshes, and along the banks of streams and ponds. To find worms, insects, small fish, and other tiny creatures in or near the water, the mole uses a strange super power. It blows bubbles through its nostrils at a rate of five to ten bubbles a second—and immediately sucks them back in. Each bubble picks up and carries the smell of any nearby animal. The scent tells the nearly blind mole whether or not the animal is safe to eat.

87 STAR-NOSED MOLES BLOW BUBBLES

*88 SWIFTS FLY NONSTOP

Swifts are the champions of migrating birds. They leave Europe late in the fall, fly all the way south to Africa, and return to Europe in the early spring. The trip is over 1,000 miles (1,609 km) long and takes 200 days. Yet these birds never touch the ground during that entire time! They catch flying insects for food to eat and skim over ponds and streams for water to drink. According to recent research, swifts do not even rest at night. They just glide along or flap their wings more slowly!

Termites build tall air-conditioned homes, or mounds, out of dirt, dung, and spit. The mounds can be the height of two-story buildings. To cool their homes, the termites leave many invisible holes in the walls. This lets the warm air inside the mound mix with the cool air entering through the wall openings. Meanwhile, cool, damp air from the enormous cellar under the mound flows up to keep the air circulating. This prevents the mound from overheating. A big job for these little insects!

#89 TERMITES AIR-CONDITION THEIR HOMES

#90 TIGER MOTHS OUTSMART BATS

Tiger moths are among the few insects that bats rarely eat. That's because the moths are able to trick the bats and escape unharmed. When bats hunt for insects, they use echolocation to find their prey. That is, they send out high-pitched clicks and listen for the clicking sounds to bounce back. But tiger moths can exactly imitate the clicks that the bats make! The moths' sounds confuse the bats' echolocation and seem to say, "Don't eat me because I have a bad taste."

Vampire bats have two very sharp, triangular-shaped front teeth. Native to Central and South America, these bats usually feed on sleeping large mammals, especially cattle and horses. Using their razor-sharp teeth, the bats puncture the skin and then lap up the blood that flows out. Vampire bats may drink their victim's blood for about thirty minutes. Yet they only take in a few tablespoons of blood before their stomachs are full and they fly away. Because bat teeth are so sharp, the punctures rarely wake the victims. They sleep through the whole thing!

91 VAMPIRE BAT TEETH CUT LIKE RAZORS

#92 VERVET MONKEYS SOUND THE ALARM

Troops of vervet monkeys have sentries, or guards, that keep watch. These sentry monkeys have a particular alarm call for each kind of enemy. When threatened, the sentry faces the approaching danger and calls out to the troop. Short, loud barks mean a leopard is near, and the monkeys scamper up trees. Low-pitched grunts warn of an eagle, and they dive into the bushes. High-pitched chattering signals a snake, and they flee. But baby cries always mean "Help!"—and the adults come running.

A viperfish lives deep in the ocean, where it is very dark. Like many other deep-sea dwellers, the predator viperfish makes its own natural light. The lights are found along the sides and bottom of its body. They make the viperfish visible in the dark ocean water. But unlike those of other creatures that live near the deep-sea bottom, the viperfish's lights flash on and off. Some say the flashing lights attract smaller prey. But others believe they help the viperfish keep in touch with other viperfish and find mates.

#93 VIPERFISH FLASH THEIR LIGHTS

#94 WALLACE'S FLYING FROGS GLIDE

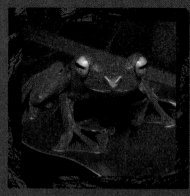

Wallace's flying frogs live in trees, coming down only to mate and lay eggs. Their super power comes from their big, wide feet—each with a web of skin between the toes. Special feet let the frogs glide without effort from tree branch to tree branch! Their feet are like wings that catch the air and support the frogs in flight. In addition, each of their toes has a special pad that allows them to make soft landings and stick to tree trunks. What those neat feet can do!

Water bears, or tardigrades, are tiny beings—each no bigger than a grain of rice! Found everywhere on the planet, these animals have experienced the very worst conditions—and survived. Researchers in labs have boiled them in water, frozen them in ice, deprived them of food and water for ten years, and even exposed them to deadly cosmic rays and airless vacuums in outer space. Yet the water bears lived on and did just fine. After a history of 500 million years on the earth, they are surely the most super-powerful animals of all time!

95 WATER BEARS DEFY DANGER

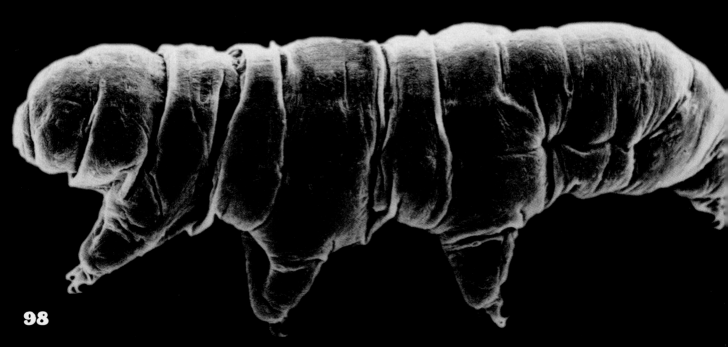

96 WATER SPIDERS BREATHE UNDERWATER

Water spiders spend their whole lives underwater—and have a really amazing way of breathing. The spider spins its web among the weeds growing in lakes, ponds, and slow-moving streams. It swims to the surface, where air bubbles stick to hairs on its body. Then it's back into the underwater web, which it fills with bubbles of air, just like balloons in a net. The water spider stays inside the web and only leaves to collect more air and to catch food.

Water striders are insects with the remarkable ability to move very quickly across water without sinking. These insects are mostly found on ponds, marshes, and streams. Tiny hairs on the ends of their feet are water repellent. That is, they do not break through the surface of the water. The hairs also trap little bubbles of air to keep the strider afloat. The front two legs are short and are mainly used to grasp prey. The four long legs carry the strider forward and help it steer.

#97 WATER STRIDERS SKATE ON WATER

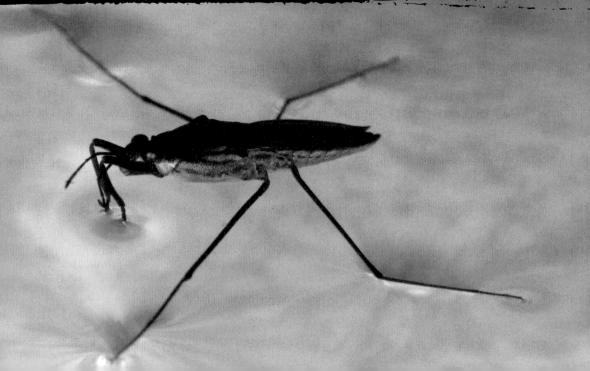

#98 WHELKS DRILL THROUGH SEASHELLS

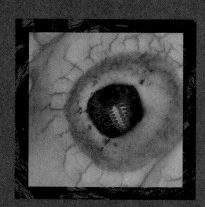

Whelks are large sea snails with spiral shells. They mostly eat mussels and clams, which are also covered with hard shells. To reach the prey's soft body inside its shell, the whelk uses a hard, tongue-like structure called a radula. The radula, which is found in a tube that extends out from the whelk's body, is covered with hundreds of small, sharp teeth. It drills holes in the victim's shell. The drilling may take two hours or more. But then the whelk gets the prey—and eats it alive!

Wolverines are the size of large dogs but are far stronger. They are fearless and willing to fight animals of any size. In the summer, they mostly eat small mammals—mice, rats, and others. But in the winter, when food is scarce, these fierce hunters prey on larger animals, such as reindeer, sheep, and moose. They especially seek animals that are weak or injured. Wolverines attack with their long, large claws and sharp teeth. They seize and chew the prey—bones and all.

99 WOLVERINES ATTACK BIG ANIMALS

100 WOLVES HOWL TO COMMUNICATE

Wolves live in groups, called packs, of one or more families. They howl to keep the pack together when separated in a thick forest or spread out over a large area. The animals share information and feelings through their howls. Wolves howl to gather for a hunt, to claim their home territory, to warn intruders away, and to identify other wolves. After a kill, the pack may howl to protect its prey from being stolen. Wolves howl for any reason—or for no reason at all!

Wood frogs survive super-cold weather by freezing. Ice forms between the cells of their body, but not inside the cells. Special antifreeze keeps the liquids in the cells from freezing and killing the frogs. While frozen, their hearts stop beating. The frogs do not breathe, and their blood does not flow. When warm weather returns, the frogs start to thaw out. Over the next few hours, heartbeat, breathing, and blood flow return to normal. It takes somewhat longer for the animals to begin moving about and feeding. And all this with no bad effects from having been frozen!

#101 WOOD FROGS FREEZE AND THAW

INDEX

PHOTO CREDITS

Nicholas J./Getty Images; 33 bottom: EEI_Tony/iStockphoto; 34 top: johnandersonphoto/iStockphoto; 34 bottom: Seapics.com; 35 top: Sascha Burkard/Shutterstock, Inc.; 35 bottom: Mark Kostich/iStockphoto; 36 top: nico99/Fotolia; 36 bottom: antpkr/Shutterstock, Inc.; 37 top: michael1959/iStockphoto; 37 bottom: Martinmark/Dreamstime; 38 top: Alex23/iStockphoto; 38 bottom: Nature Picture Library/Alamy Images; 39 top: 4FR/iStockphoto; 39 bottom: Suzi Eszterhas/Getty Images; 40 top: James Robinson/Animals Animals; 40 bottom: Nancy Nehring/iStockphoto; 41 top: VKuzmin/Thinkstock; 41 bottom: PaulReevesPhotography/Thinkstock; 42 top: R. Koenig/age fotostock; 42 bottom: drewa/iStockphoto; 43 top: Karl H. Switak/Science Source; 43 bottom: Paul Freed/age fotostock; 44 top: Norbert Probst/imageBroker/age fotostock; 44 bottom: Mary Katherine Wynn/Dreamstime; 45 top: Michael Dietrich/imageBroker/age fotostock; 45 bottom: Photoshot Holdings Ltd/Alamy Images; 46 top: Flip de Nooyer/Minden Pictures/Corbis Images; 46 bottom: Mark Bowler/Photoshot; 47 top: Matt Jeppson/Shutterstock, Inc.; 47 bottom: Gilbert S Grant/Getty Images; 48 top: National Geographic Image Collection/Alamy Images; 48 bottom: DEA Picture Library/age fotostock; 49 top: Suzi Eszterhas/Getty Images; 49 bottom: imageBroker/Alamy Images; 50 top: Tom Tietz/Getty Images; 50 bottom: John Cancalosi/Nature Picture Library; 51 top: Patricia Hofmeester/Dreamstime; 51 bottom: Konrad Wothe/LOOK-foto/Getty Images; 52 top: drferry/Thinkstock; 52 bottom: phakimata/Thinkstock; 53 top: kenglye/iStockphoto; 53 bottom: mtilboe5/Thinkstock; 54 top: Jayone1981/Dreamstime; 54 bottom: zahoor salmi/Getty Images; 55 top: CoreyFord/iStockphoto; 55 bottom: Protasov AN/Shutterstock, Inc.; 56 top: opzjon/iStockphoto; 56 bottom: Kram1975/Shutterstock, Inc.; 57 top: keitchink/iStockphoto; 57 bottom: webstuff/iStockphoto; 58 top: Joakim Leroy/iStockphoto; 58 bottom: Anna Kucherova/iStockphoto; 59 top: Craig Dingle/iStockphoto; 59 bottom: Craig Dingle/iStockphoto; 60 top: John Anderson/Thinkstock; 60 bottom: WaterFrame/Alamy Images; 61 top: Charlie Edward/Shutterstock, Inc.; 61 bottom: Ryan M. Bolton/Shutterstock, Inc.; 62 top: Feathercollector/Dreamstime; 62 bottom: Piotr Naskrecki/Minden Pictures; 63 top: Aquanaut4/Dreamstime; 63 bottom: Aquanaut4/Dreamstime; 64 top: Auscape / UIG/Getty Images; 64 bottom: David Maitland/Getty Images; 65 top: Seapics.com; 65 bottom: Seapics.com; 66 top: Mans Photo/Shutterstock, Inc.; 66 bottom: David Fleetham/Alamy Images; 67 top: imageBroker/Alamy Images; 67 bottom: Digdam Sean Casper/Dreamstime; 68 top: Ian Vrbsicka/Dreamstime; 68 bottom: Ardea/Jim Zipp/ Animals Animals; 69 top: blickwinkel/Alamy Images; 69 bottom: blueband/Shutterstock, Inc.; 70 top: Fred Bavendam/Minden Pictures/Corbis Images; 70 bottom: FLPA/D P Wilson/age fotostock; 71 top: Dante Fenolio/Getty Images; 71 bottom: Gregory G. Dimijian/Science Source; 72 top: AndreaBovolo/iStockphoto; 72 bottom: TOM MCHUGH/Getty Images; 73 top: ElliotHurwitt/Thinkstock; 73 bottom: moodboard/Thinkstock; 74 bottom: Lynn Bystrom/Dreamstime; 74 top: bydlife/iStockphoto; 75 top: Guy Sagi/Thinkstock; 75 bottom: Dennis Donohue/iStockphoto; 76 top: Hans Reinhard/Science Source; 76 bottom: blickwinkel/Alamy Images; 77 top: Renaud Visage/Thinkstock; 77 bottom: ArminStautBerlin/Thinkstock; 78 top: Rivertrail/Dreamstime; 78 bottom: Cata37/Dreamstime; 79 top: Sannydaez/Dreamstime; 79 bottom: Steven van Soldt/iStockphoto; 80 top: Jill Lang/Shutterstock, Inc.; 80 bottom: Seapics; 81 top: ShaneKato/iStockphoto; 81 bottom: Greg Amptman/Dreamstime; 82 top: GlobalP/Getty Images; 82 bottom: Eric Isselee/Shutterstock, Inc.; 83 top: Mark Kostich/iStockphoto; 83 bottom: taviphoto/Shutterstock, Inc.; 84 top, 84 bottom: Seapics.com; 85 top: LionH/iStockphoto; 85 bottom: Cathy Keifer/Dreamstime; 86 top: Stephen Dalton/Minden Pictures; 86 bottom: Nature Picture Library/Alamy Images; 87 top: yogesh more/iStockphoto; 87 bottom: Orionmystery/Dreamstime; 88 top: Narchuk/Shutterstock, Inc.; 88 bottom: Seapics.com; 89 top: Ross Kinne/ Animals Animals; 89 bottom: Zigmund Leszczynski/Animals Animals; 90 top: Ken Catania/Visuals Unlimited/Corbis Images; 90 bottom: Visuals Unlimited, Inc./Ken Catania/Getty Images; 91 top: blickwinkel/Alamy Images; 91 bottom: Floriana/Fotolia; 92 top: Sutichak/Dreamstime; 92 bottom: ElenaNic/iStockphoto; 93 top: Michael Durham/Getty Images; 93 bottom: Jaquex/Shutterstock, Inc.; 94 top: Ardea/Nick Gordon/ Animals Animals; 94 bottom: Ardea/Nick Gordon/ Animals Animals; 95 top: SouWest Photography/Shutterstock, Inc.; 95 bottom: Impalastock/iStockphoto; 96 top: Seapics.com; 96 bottom: Danté Fenolio/Science Source; 97 top left: Nature Picture Library/Alamy; 97 bottom: Image Quest Marine/Alamy Images; 98 top: Science Photo Library/Alamy Images; 98 bottom: Dr. Diane R. Nelson/Getty Images; 99 top: Wildlife GmbH/Alamy Images; 99 bottom: D. Kucharski K. Kucharska/Shutterstock, Inc.; 100 top: WebSubstance/iStockphoto; 100 bottom: 3MJ/Shutterstock, Inc.; 101 top: blickwinkel/Alamy Images; 101 bottom: Seapics.com; 102 top: Michal Ninger/Shutterstock, Inc.; 102 bottom: Lukas Blazek/Dreamstime; 103 top: Peter Weimann/Animals Animals; 103 bottom: Edwin Butter/Shutterstock, Inc.; 104 top: EVAfoto/iStockphoto; 104 bottom: Ted Kinsman/Science Source; 112 top: Arenacreative/Dreamstime; 112 bottom: drferry/Thinkstock.

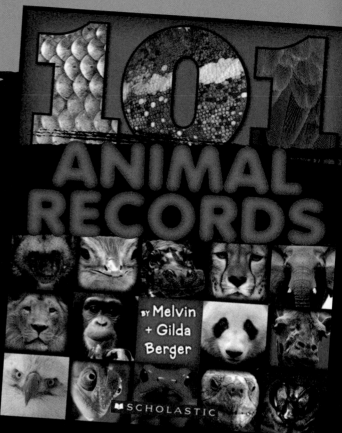

101 FREAKY ANIMALS

BY Melvin + Gilda Berger

SCHOLASTIC

101 ANIMAL babies

BY Melvin + Gilda Berger

SCHOLASTIC

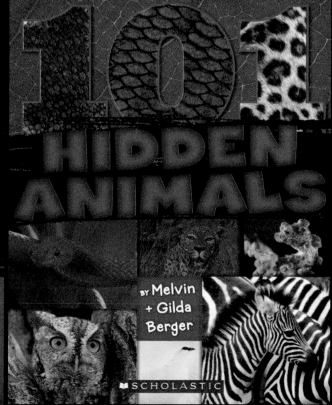

101 HIDDEN ANIMALS

BY Melvin + Gilda Berger

SCHOLASTIC

ABOUT THE AUTHORS

MELVIN AND GILDA BERGER are the authors of more than two hundred books for children. Their books have received awards from the National Science Teachers Association, the Library of Congress, and the New York Public Library. The Bergers live in New York.